This Bird Can't Fly

Susan Canizares • Daniel Moreton

Scholastic Inc.

New York • Toronto • London • Auckland • Sydney

Acknowledgments

Science Consultants: Patrick R. Thomas, Ph.D., Bronx Zoo/Wildlife Conservation Park;
Glenn Phillips, The New York Botanical Garden
Literacy Specialist: Ada Cordova, District 2, New York City

Design: MKR Design, Inc.

Photo Research: Barbara Scott

Endnotes: Samantha Berger

Endnote Illustrations: Craig Spearing

Photographs: Cover: Gordon Wiltsie/Peter Arnold; p. 1&2: Johnny Johnson/DRK
Photo; p. 3: Martin Harvey/NHPA; p. 4: Clem Haagner/PhotoResearchers;
p. 5: Fred Bruemmer/Peter Arnold; p. 6: R Van Nostrand/Photo
Researchers; p. 7: Gordon Wiltsie/Peter Arnold; p. 8: Johnny Johnson/DRK
Photo; p. 9: Martin Wendler/Peter Arnold; p. 10: Frank W Lane/Bruce
Colman; p. 11: Johnny Johnson/DRK Photo; p. 12: Tim Davis/Photo Researchers

Library of Congress Cataloging-in-Publication Data
Canizares, Susan
This bird can't fly / Susan Canizares, Daniel Moreton.
p. cm. -- (Science emergent readers)
Includes index.
Summary: Simple text and photographs show how the penguin,
ostrich, and other flightless birds can travel by swimming, running,
sliding, and other methods of movement.
ISBN 0-590-76968-5 (pbk.: alk. paper)
1. Flightless birds--Juvenile literature. [1. Flightless birds. 2. Birds.]
I. Moreton, Daniel. II. Title. III. Series
QL676.2.C355   1998
598.147'9--dc21   98-18823
                                                                         CIP AC

30 29 28 27 26 25 24 23 22 21 20 19 18   08   10 11 12 13 14 15/0

This bird can't fly,

but it can slide.

This bird can't fly,

but it can fight.

This bird can't fly,

but it can swim.

This bird can't fly,

but it can dive.

This bird can't fly,

but it can run.

This bird can't fly,

but it has fun!

This Bird Can't Fly

Although all birds have wings, more than 20 types of bird cannot fly! Long ago, certain birds, who did not need to fly away from predators or to search for food, gradually lost their ability to fly.

The emperor penguin (pages 1–2) uses its paddle-like wings to swim and slide rather than fly. Its stiff wings help it to dive and propel itself through the water with great ease. Penguins move much more quickly swimming in water than waddling on land. One way they move more quickly on land is by pushing themselves on their bellies over the ice. This way of traveling is called toboganning.

The ostrich (pages 3–4), the largest living bird today, is a member of a group of flightless birds called ratites. Instead of flying to flee from danger, ratites run on their long, strong legs. Faster than any other two-legged animal, ostriches can run up to 40 miles an hour! They have only two toes, unlike other birds, which have four. They have a long, very sharp pointed toenail on each foot, which they use as weapons when fighting. Ostriches can also kick extremely hard to defend themselves.

Although most water fowl can fly, three out of four kinds of steamer duck (pages 5–6) cannot. The muscles in their wings aren't developed enough for flying, but they are able to flap them very quickly. Flapping over the water with their wings — and paddling with their webbed feet — allows steamer ducks to swim remarkably fast.

Adelie penguins (pages 7–8), like the emperor, toboggan as a means of locomotion. They can often be found diving, one after the next, like a group of synchronized swimmers. When they dive and swim together as a group, they have more protection from predators in the sea.

Rheas (pages 9–10), like ostriches, are ratites, and can run incredibly quickly. Running from danger can be just as good an escape as flying. Rheas can run faster than horses, if need be, and can swim as well! Their hearing and eyesight are so sharp that other animals often stay close to them for protection. These animals know that if a group of rheas suddenly begins to run, danger may be approaching and they had better run too!

King penguins (pages 11–12) are able to dive deeper than any other penguin. The record thus far is 1,060 feet down! Like all penguins, they have wing bones that are fused together to form stiff paddles, which are excellent for locomotion under water. They use their webbed feet, beak, and tail to steer when swimming and their flipper-wings for balance and forward momentum.

Birds that cannot fly can survive in their habitats just as well as birds that can. Although they cannot take to the air for flight, look at all the things they can do!